Volume 76 of the Yale Series of Younger Poets

GREEN
SOLDIERS

JOHN BENSKO

FOREWORD BY RICHARD HUGO

NEW HAVEN AND LONDON, YALE UNIVERSITY PRESS

*Published with assistance from
the Mary Cady Tew Memorial Fund*

*Designed by Sally Harris
and set in Zapf International type.
Printed in the United States of America by
The Alpine Press, South Braintree, Mass.*

Library of Congress Cataloging in Publication Data

Bensko, John, 1949–
   Green soldiers.

   (Yale series of younger poets; v. 76)
   I. Title. II. Series.
PS3552.E547655G7   811'.54   80-26052
ISBN 0-300-02637-4
ISBN 0-300-02644-7 (pbk.)

10 9 8 7 6 5 4 3 2 1

FOR TOM RABBITT

Contents

Foreword

One reason that psychoanalysis succeeds is because we are the stories we tell. If the narrator is internal, we tell, and consequently are, the stories we hear. From his internal narrator, John Bensko has heard a lot of stories about people who died before he was born. Ultimately, the people who stock his fictions and the poems that grow from those fictions, through some poetic alchemy, become so immediately related to Bensko and to ourselves that they rightfully can be called ancestors.

The first section of John Bensko's book is filled with ancestors. In it, part of that poetic alchemy involves the psychological trick of reproducing immediacy by pinpointing the irrelevant detail that mysteriously remains a part of the total (often awful) experience imagined decades later.

> Beside the dressing station two nurses
> pull a sheet over a man blown to pieces.
> The wind ruffles their skirts.
>
> ["Troop Train"]

The opening poem, "Garcia Lorca and the One-legged Schoolteacher," is one of the few poems not based on a privately constructed fiction but, in this case, on a published account of the execution of Lorca (who barely appears in the poem). Both the priest and Lorca could be our ancestors, the one trying to keep alive his best impulses in a world where good impulses are hopelessly out of place, the other doomed to die unnoticed in a world diverted by hard circumstance from the values his deep human dedication gave that world. Perhaps our most recognizable ancestors are the "men" who "notice" that

> . . . you live with one leg
> and your death spreads,

and the "children" who spread the mythic proportions of
death

> when one of them finds a dead rabbit
> and brings it in a sack to school.

Through his fictions Bensko creates a world where events are
meaningless and the human consequences enormous—not
insistently enormous in the poems themselves but enormous
in some telling personal way in the mind of the reader.

Part of the technique involves Bensko's being the fictions
he creates: while his relations with his "ancestors," as I prefer
to call them, seem impersonal, he still reveals his inner self,
as if he must deny feeling to express it. Bensko feels love is
the opposite of fascination ("Troop Train") and that reducing
events to fundamental descriptive details ("Navarre Beach,"
"France and the Return") defines the tradition of futility passed
down directly from our forebears. Suffering is thicker than
blood and pain creates its own genetic structure.

The trilogy, "The Lovers," presents three victims of love and
circumstance. "Herr Steinmann" though he miraculously es-
capes from the Germans, nonetheless loses not only his wife
but also his ability to create. He is a victim of World War II
and stays alive only on memories. "Marie" has also escaped
the Nazis. She finds herself so crippled by a lover's deceit that
she must live in a world where language is of little or no
consequence and survival depends on the willful distortion
of the past, on not responding to what goes on around her.
The man in "The Trout Stream," perhaps an ex-German sol-
dier, is now the victim of a bad marriage. His feelings may
well be Bensko's:

> What is safe is nothing: a memory,
> a paralysis. . . .

Bensko shows a constant distrust of real experience, and perhaps his poems are an effort to find himself a place in a world where too much can happen. His poems could well be an effort to accept a world of grim experience without the attendant bitterness and anguish of those who have lived it.

Two poems are strategically placed in the book. "A Veteran of the Great War," appears at the end of the first section; and "The Night-blooming Cactus," is at the end of the second section, the end of the book. The opening line of "A Veteran of the Great War":

> It all seems like today: he returns

could be said of any number of poems in the book. This poem is based on the idea that if you tell stories well enough, often enough, even if the stories become confused with others, all the important elements will find their rightful places. It's a matter of narrating (or rather lying) with such immediacy that the "facts" become true in the mind and open new poetic possibilities.

A man suffering from a World War I gas attack returns home to find his father dead and his aunt, for whom he has erotic feelings, alone in the house. Following an incestuous affair, the aunt leaves. "Later, he confuses the story," and renders her one of two skeletons, "two friends," from the war, found over thirty years later buried in a trench. This new fiction, found suddenly in the poem, provides the veteran the opportunity for a pun:

> I had an aunt in the Great War, he says.

Time becomes telescoped by the end of the poem: "earlier in the day," is the day over forty years ago that started the poem.

The veteran still suffers from the effects of the enemy gas, and he still tells "stories in which every day / is today." His life, estimated to last six months after the war, has gone on for decades. Portraits become real people. The veteran tells stories to neighborhood children and shares their childlike belief in the value and reality of the immediacy of fiction. Bensko's poems are appealing because in reading them we become children. We must, in order to truly understand them.

"The Night-blooming Cactus" illuminates Bensko's unusual method of locating and writing (recording, almost) poems. By concentrating, through "the love and the meditation" that "go on," the man in the poem is able to become the cactus, and later he is able to transmute the absent girl he is trying to understand into the cactus. Converting himself and the girl into the cactus parallels converting concern into a conviction that he "cares for nothing," the girl means nothing, the colors of the cactus mean nothing, and the girl feels nothing. Bensko appears best able to transfer his private feelings into words when he's convinced the subject of his attention feels nothing for him and he feels nothing for it. In other words, Bensko has a profound faith in the moral and emotional neutrality of the imagination. Once a poet can escape those feelings that demand traditional loyalties, he can play with thoughts and words in ways that will enable him to go beyond limitations imposed by truth, fidelity to fact, and moral and emotional commitments necessary to making one's way in the everyday world.

The second section of the book, while still rooted in fictions, involves up-to-date scenes and, in a way, parts of Bensko's own life. Some of those parts are fictions themselves. A prolonged critical study would trace an ancestral lineage from parents in the first section of the book to their descendants in the second. The psychotic soldier in "Recovering" could be the great grandfather of the boy who gratuitously and instinctively kills the toad in "The Survivor." The woman at Amiens who stood helpless while "her soldier" went off across the bridge, one of the doomed many, could well be the grandmother of the senile mother-in-law in "To My Wife." Unfolding from those fictions are poems so haunting, the fictions deserve to be called supreme.

It is impossible to distinguish fact from fiction or reality from imagination in Bensko's poems, which is all to his credit. Any good storyteller knows that stories actually *do* improve with age. Improve because the narrator tells them better and better. Bensko's poems build age into the stories and at the same time keep the stories fresh and new. It's impossible not to believe them. Like our dreams and our lives, the more we modify our stories with memory, the more we polish them with narrative technique and with visual replay, the more vivid and real they become. John Bensko is a poet of the vivid and the real. Like each of us, he is a veteran of a great war, and he has the poems to prove it.

Richard Hugo

Acknowledgments

Acknowledgment is made to the following publications for poems which originally appeared in them.

The Black Warrior Review: "Garcia Lorca and the One-legged Schoolteacher"
Carolina Quarterly: "The Pet Cat"
Critical Quarterly: "Navarre Beach"
Intro 10: "Mrs. McCullen"
New Orleans Review: "To My Wife"
Poetry Northwest: "A Last Look in the Sambre Canal," "A Veteran of the Great War," "The Children's Committee," and "The Trout Stream" (from "The Lovers")
Prairie Schooner: "Mail Call," "The Young Woman at Amiens: 1914"

I

Garcia Lorca and the
One-legged Schoolteacher

No one sings here,
* no one cries in the corner.*

The luck of an old priest.
He wins a morning's sleep
because he believes:

today no one will be executed.

He sleeps a mile away
from the hill
where they shoot people.

He hears only bells
against the wind
and dreams

of the fountain and the boy
herding goats at dawn.

To Fuente Grande and the olive grove,
to the fountain filled with goat bells.

In the roadhouse the poet and Gonzalez,
the one-legged schoolteacher, waste
their last minutes arguing
with guards who must kill them.

There will be no confessions.

Now the sleeping priest
dreams a trumpet
and shots in the distance.

Now three soldiers
as young and soft as angels
empty their pistols
in the soft necks of gourds.

The sun shifts along the hill
and lights up the grey shale.

The priest waking
believes the shots have come

because of the laughter and the beauty
of girls. He goes to the fountain
and hears from the boy he loves:

how he watched two girls bathe
under the shade of the olive trees;

how he heard flies and cried,
recognizing the one leg
of the dead schoolteacher.

The priest hears the goat bells
and dips his hand in the waters.
He thinks of the kindest words:

God forgives
those who die under olive trees.

What men notice, he thinks,
is you live with one leg
and your death spreads,

like the buzz of children
when one of them finds a dead rabbit
and brings it in a sack to school.

The Boy with the Frightened Horse

Alain, they say, Alain
get away from the tracks
or you'll be killed.
The foggy Belgian woods
are dim tonight.
The lights in the train windows
flash in and out
like a string of fireflies.
A night like this
his brothers left for the war.
He tightens the reins
to calm his frightened horse.
The engine rumbles
and shakes his feet.

Officers come out for air.
In full brass and medals
they are like kings
going up and down.
New recruits
crowd past them to the cars.
They tease the boy.
Alain, they say,
why don't you tie your horse
and come with us?
Over enemy guns
he would charge the top.
The green field of battle
explodes
with horses and bright flags.

The last car pulling out
is past his dreams:
gold lions parade down the sides
of the royal parlor car.
It must be a king.
It's a king, he shouts.
The others rush to look
as the train
churns into the fog.
Alain, they say,
did you see him? Did you see him?
The boy gives them nothing.
He is frozen in salute,
his frightened horse
ready for battle.
The pale and confused Negro,
alone on the last car,
returns to sleep.

Missed Connections

At noon there's a whistle in the distance.
The tracks go out of sight, wavering
in the heat across the flats.

It's Sunday. For the afternoon, some men
stand in circles on the railroad platform.
Their women sit on benches along the wall.
The children are playing with a stray dog.

The brown terrier barks and runs in circles
refusing to chase the stick across the tracks.
A boy throws the stick and hits an old drunk
who picks it up and walks closer.

Again, there's the whistle in the distance.
The boy's father tells the drunk
to get lost. The others turn and close in.

The drunk explains: all he wants is some work.
I can sing, he says. He can sing.
His head tilts back and the old tune
breaks into the dry afternoon.

The train rumbles down the tracks.
The town drifts in. The terrier pinwheels
in the dust like a tornado.
Faces in the windows move past.

The whistle drops pitch in the distance.
Sleepy and ignored, the drunk still sings.

Troop Train

The survivors for the front regret their wounds
weren't enough. The train pulls out.
Beside the dressing station two nurses
pull a sheet over a man blown to pieces.
The wind ruffles their skirts.

In the aisle a bandaged arm here, a leg
there, dangle like cloth. A sergeant
coming back from rest, he says, home
to the front, unrolls a print of a French girl
and tells the others: spies are everywhere.

He offers some wine
and says how good it feels to be going home
where, if he is taken for granted,
it is because he is loved. He handles
a photo from his pocket, a wife smiling
and a girl whose delicate body balances
on a tree limb, like china, a rare souvenir.

A green soldier lifts his suprised
face out of a sack and wipes his mouth. Home?
he says, I think we're going to the front.
A man down the aisle goes into a fit.
He believes the countryside has turned to fire.
The sergeant is calm, staring into his wife.
Deceit, he says. Love and deceit.

No one hears him. Their heads are leaning
into the aisle, wrapped up in the story
of the fire and the faceless man who has survived it.
I live with them, the sergeant says.
I take them for granted.

The Young Woman at Amiens: 1914

One of the last soldiers leaving across the bridge
is her soldier: a bright, silver spoon
stuck in his cap. Last night she told him
she would never take her eyes off him.
She did not expect the oak tree. The movement
of thousands of dark birds is like one creature.

One day when she was a small girl
her grandmother took her to a grove of trees
where crows had been roosting for centuries.
The ground was almost white.
One crow made a sound like a baby.

The cold night her brother showed her
the hedgerow alive with birds,
she clapped her hands.
Birds shot out, like an explosion
shattering the ice on the leaves.

This morning there is ice in all the trees.
She looks again at the bridge, the soldiers.
Hers is just a boy, a hand waving,
a bright spoon going off in the distance.

The Park Bench

We watch the far side of the lake.
The beginnings of rain and wind
brush the surface.
Here, the ducks stretch their necks

and spread their wings.
Sarah, they are not interested in you.
We have watched too long.
Too many young girls have tried it.

When you kneel on the sidewalk
and tempt the ducks with corn
you are nearly beautiful.
They will bruise

your fingers and put out your eyes.
Smell their feathers, dry
and inviting as a pillow?
They are stiff and sharp.

We have been here long enough.
We know you will become
breathless as you follow
their flight into the rain.

And we have watched you
and that young gentleman
stroll barefoot
on the muddy shore.

The next evening as you gazed
from the pier alone
that black and white terrier of yours
was nipping at our heels.

Sarah, we have taken the time.
We have talked it over.
Some girls shouldn't hope
to marry well.

Recovering

Fleurs-de-lis wallpaper the hall.
The lilies mock me everywhere.
At Neuve-Chapelle the shrapnel
left a star in my skull.
Lily the nurse wants to know
why all the trees have leaves
like spikes of palms.

The valley looked like a desert.
The trees were shattered
and water filled the craters.
At an oasis men from both sides
lounged on the green.
How many times a night
do you see this? How many times
a day? A gold fleur-de-lis
patterns itself across her white blouse.

They are wallpapering her chest.
She won't listen.
How many times? Have put numbers
on my clothes. Move when I move.
I tell her, *these* are the only answers:
The room has a window. The room has a chest.
Fill it with numbers of the very best.
Friend is Jack, brother is Mark,
the man with no arms screams in the dark.

They are taking down the road signs.
They are putting fleurs-de-lis on the door,
on the windows, along the floor

like footprints leaving.
Lily refuses to believe.
What can I do?
Convince her: palm trees,
numbers. All we have, all we have
between us are these.

Navarre Beach

Because the boy went swimming when
the tide was strong, and felt the water slip
under his feet and take him down, the pain
of his lungs struggled past hope.
His fear was simply gone,
a basic want like love and hunger. Air
became water, filling his last desire.

Because days later we were the crowd
fishing at the pier, we watched the log
float in and become a splotched body, the drowned
boy lying on the sand. The dog
and the children saw it calmly. Water drained
from his mouth and made most of us turn,
sick at the sight of his return.

We want to give him to someone who cares.
Because, in description, it is simple.
A neat package done up in plastic.
He waits in the sun.

A Last Look in the Sambre Canal

for Wilfred Owen

The bells of the Armistice wake his family.
The girls put on their best ribbons and sing
while they shake his clothes in the window.
When his mother comes back from the post and drops
the letter in the ditch, she understands

the sound of guns, the duckboards wet
and covered with mud, and the difficulty
of carrying anything, a letter, a poem, across
the canal and into the house. The letter fades
the way his body drifts,

plum and green and luxuriant in the water
with a charm that stops the guns. Like their farm
in Kent he'll sprout violets and moss. His face
rises in the water with a smile accustomed
to a world turning itself green.

The news of his death arrived in England
days after the war ended and the Sambre peasants
picked him clean of souvenirs. On the dresser
in his mother's house his last photo,
a notebook, and a drawing come to light.

In the shade of the few trees left, his body
stalls, poems float from his pockets
and his eyes follow them. What do the words
reflect? A letter, his mother, the girls singing?
The water, more than a mirror, dissolves them.

The Gypsies

Crows wheel and caw.
The lazy strokes of the irrigation jets
mist into green rows.
The foreman's arm waves
an arc of red bandana, meaning
pick up the pace. It is time for lunch.
He is tired of flies
and bored, and a little crazy in the hot sun.

The gypsy woman's fingers dig
at the base of the cabbage.
She is through with his clever talk,
with rainbows
trailing away and coming back.
The dusty road
is full of holes, leading out.
The crows and flies will not touch her.

Her fingers dig at the white, stringy roots
until they churn to dirt.
the field greens and blackens
and fades like the photo
of her husband.
Lost in the well for days
his face is battered and swollen.
His wet hair is lapped up.

His uncontrollable, happy dog
daydreams in the hot sun.
Daydreams of the foreman wiping his brow
while holding a clutch of flowers.

They are red, and yellow, and violet.
He is saying remember me.
He is suggesting rainbows in the hot sun,
another night, and his dank, lovely room.

The Lovers

I. Herr Steinmann

He knows her body is impossible
to find in stone. He knew it the afternoon
his model held her breasts, wanting him.
It's the war, he thinks, the war moves things.
Outside his studio the soldiers goosestep
across the bridge into fog. The Jews
with bandanas on their faces have shoveled
the last starved child onto their wagon.
His model, like a child, is not a child.
Later, when the Gestapo comes
to get them, he is squatting on the floor,
starved until he's eating rocks and chalk.
A few commands are snapped. He answers
a question, wrong, and then he's in the woods
standing with some old Jews waiting for a message.
For some food. Or a truck to take them somewhere.
One thinks he's a tree. We can stay alive, he whispers,
hidden in the deep leaves and the others.

In the leaves of the forest outside Dresden
the body of Eva Steinmann is grey
and angular as the stone carvings of her.
A smear of chalk on her lips is all
that's left of her lover. He's miles away
from the rifle shots picking out the last Jews.
He's past the river and the border guards,
the miles when his hands were quick enough
to catch lizards for food. He's alone
leaning against the wall of his garden.

It's evening in America. With chalk he tries
to draw the outline of a girl, then
another. But the wall is covered with chalk.
In the shadows a small chameleon is frozen
against the bricks. For a moment the man feels
how all things, the garden, the lizard, the cold
body of Eva Steinmann, point to his death.
But I'm not dead, he says. And he remembers how it was
to be young, and hungry, and resting in the leaves.

II. Marie

At dusk children come down to dig for clams
along the bottom of the sea wall. As far back
around the island as she can see them
shore birds are pecking the mud for food.
She finds a break in the wall and waits for the tide.
She has with her the book of poems
in which her husband lied about loving her.
For him, Mont-Saint-Michel was unreachable,
the symbol for their love. And now, for her, escaping
Paris, the Nazis, it becomes exile,
distant and impossible as he described it:

the forest around the island of Mont-Saint-Michel,
the tired knight riding from the trees at dusk,
and the saint who walks through the trees,
wearing birds under the long shadows of morning,
have been lost for centuries. She hears
the antique, wavering voice of a monk
climbing into his Aves. The cool night air
drains her from her loss.

His cruel face the last time they made love
is beauty she thinks she understands.
Washed of its trees by the salt and wind

the rocks of Mont-Saint-Michel,
the monastery and the stone village,
can't compare to the forest
sprouting green from the grey mud.
The children are gone who dug holes
across the flats, gathering baskets of clams.
She thinks how children in the fairy tale
became lost. They drowned in the green
of a forest too deep for words.

Turning in the dark by her side,
turning and saying it straight to her face,
even though he couldn't see her face,
how could he lie about wanting her?
Under the moon the rocks of the mountain
are gold. The monk is climbing.
The children will return.
And still, she closes her eyes
and doesn't listen. She imagines the forest,
the wind in the green leaves,
and her lover, like a child, and beautiful,

the years they lose wandering in the trees.

III. *The Trout Stream*

"In Autumn the red and yellow leaves
on the clear stream wash the rocks. The trout
flicks its tail and hangs beside a sunken log."

His wife's voice across the water
is that song about marching to heaven.
He thinks of Germany and the war.
The young nun from the convent
hangs her clothes in the limbs
and bathes in the river.

All night he has followed a star
hanging at dawn like a bright fly
over the water. The wind blows seeds across
like parasols and the girl catches them
and presses them to her breast.
He remembers wading into the river.
A bright yellow fly
falls like a star.

The war and the girl with the parasol
at her breast are another life.
When he comes back to her each day she is
transformed, the faces, the voices of a house
full of children. One learns too late
her language is wrong and the star
is a planet leading the wrong way.
What is safe is nothing: a memory,
a paralysis. The trout stream numbs
his legs, the cold fun of the catch.

Years ago his father showed him
a deep pool where a big trout was gliding
just under the surface.
His fly hit the water and the trout struck.
There was a moment the fish stopped midair
flushed with dark spots
before it fell exhausted on the rocks.
It was easy to forget everything
except the stream, the woods and the fresh air.
He thought he could live like that.

Downcurrent his wife finds a deep pool.
She walks into the water, into the shade
where her body almost disappears.
He casts the line and works the fly.
The trout floats into the light,

half dark and half silver. It strikes.
The line brings a kind of song from the water,
more like whistling when the fish struggles.
The life in it grows tired.
The trout jumps.
For a moment clear out of the water
it is as free as anything.

Mrs. McCullen

I never let you touch me because
you are not strong enough to forget.
The farmhouse and that sleeping girl
were suddenly lighted by the moon
lifting its stare into the window.
Is it my fault you told me too much?

Night after night her face is more beautiful,
distant, and impossible. I think nothing
escapes you. On the morning you left her
and returned to the war, there were men
singing on the road. There was a woman in a green dress
who begged for food and told you

the next morning there would be ice in the trees.
Nothing mattered but the girl.
That pack of dogs tearing at the dead horse
was spattered with blood and flies.
What you couldn't see, you imagined:
Mars, bright and red, leading you on to war.

You had to tell me so I'd feel it.
The girl's lips were softer than mine.
When you bend to kiss me and my lips form
the words . . . . No, I say, I won't; I see
your hands; coward across the sheets.
To the moon, to the girl. In the morning

I watch Mars, a small, red dot
coming through the tree outside our window.
How far will I let you go, I wonder,
before I let you touch me?

A Baby in the House

A few days into spring when the sun
warms the house, and the girl's mother
shuts a window to exclude the smell
of flowers and new grass,
she decides on something rotten
and suspects a dead cat in the wall.
Upstairs the girl's father,
who is always rethinking the Great War,
enters the French woods and discovers
a dead horse smouldering in a fire.
The girl, who lived in the room,
sits in her kitchen in another town,
daydreaming the smell of coffee.

Later in the day she will open a newspaper
and mistake a photo for her parents
standing in her room full of broken plaster.
Her father has an axe,
poised before he chops into the baby.
She reads the story and realizes:
two firemen are saving some children.
One must have a reason, she thinks,
and looks at her flower box
which flares harmlessly beyond the window.
You're crazy, she says, meaning her parents.

The Drunken Landlord

For once it is not our fault
and the landlady knows it.
In the stairwell her husband's nude body
hangs by one foot from the skylight.

Is he? Should we?
Spit drops from his mouth,
not blood. He is only
passed out for the day.

The wooden slats of the skylight
twist and creak, the weight
of the noose, his purple foot.
Sun and clouds through the window.

Our faces blush and pale
under his dangerous nudity. Our arms
are the useless net
he will fall through.

How long will he last?
The paint snaps off the skylight
in big flakes. The glass
will shatter and blind us.

Should we call the police?
Will the fire department come?

Brush his hair with your broom.
Give us the room to climb.

Can we cut? Are you sure?
We might as well, while we're at it,
ask about the heat,
and why the pipes clang at night.

Mail Call

He expects the old names to return
in the haze of rain through the garden trees
interrupted by his wife setting down coffee
with the morning mail. Even when rain
smears their letters to purple and green, he knows

who they are. The rain stops. The sun is bright.
He is walking down the trench to collect the mail.
All is well. The smells of food and coffee are
nearly enough to cover the rot. The boys
mark their postcards. "I am fine" means

I am at the front. Those at home never understand.
He wants to take the cards and erase them.
A shout, a machine gun, the sounds of feet
across the wire almost on him.
He jumps to the light and scans the shattered trees.

The trees are blasted. The brick wall of the garden
is an enemy plan, a confusion, a reminder of home.
Then it's years later and he is looking beyond it
into the sun. For a moment the pain and blindness
bring together the two codes: the one

his wife sees, the other in which all life
is point blank, the enemy guns,
the bright sun on the day of battle
and postcards home for the dead,
the instinct of their hands to block out pain.

France and the Return

In the last letter from his wife, two days
before her ship returns from France,
she describes blue sky and birds. Hundreds
flush into the air after hunters fire.

For her the memory is like their frozen field,
trees blown out of their roots, her husband
with dynamite. After the blackbirds flash
in the limbs, the sound of thunder stalls.

The green dial of the radar
sweeps the Atlantic. The letter goes on: a mountainside,
men working in a field, how it feels to walk
through a vineyard with the small, sweet

grapes fermenting on the ground. The ship's key
answers . . . yesterday, at noon, stop.
The rest escapes. At the dock
when they unload her, she is packed in ice.

She wears the perfume of her letter.
Like one of their old misunderstandings:
his hand moves out of habit.
He shades her eyes from the sun.

The Midnight Sun

Someone has taken him in his rocking chair
to the mountains where a cold lake
opens the snow like a blue, startled mouth.
He has forgotten her name.
So he invents one: Inga, the woman
who keeps him company for years.
This evening from the dining room
he watches the blackbirds peck the strawberries
she throws for them; the fourth day
the sun has refused to set by midnight.
The red berries sink in the snow.

Inga, what is it? The way she goes on
beyond the window, talking to the birds in sounds
that mean as little as anything. *Why are you
throwing strawberries for blackbirds?
Who am I?* An old doctor
listening to the lies of women and birds.
Inga, he remembers. Inga was his wife.
The sun is the lie she shares with him
to keep quiet about dying. The sun
in the lake is like a candle guttering
in blue wax. He waits, lost in the difference.

The Bones of Lazarus

"All the time we knew his corpse was rotting,
unseen as those things should be, wrapped in sheets."

But we let the old man go on
and walk among our children,
talking to the birds and animals.

We loved him and we decided he was harmless.
A penny here, a penny there.
So he went on for years.

His hands shook a little, and he was sometimes
forgetful, stumbling into the room
when he wasn't wanted. We ignored his failures.

Because we knew by then
age had taken its course. Only bones
were left. It was then he died.

That night we washed him. The bones
rode easily under the dried, yellow skin.
We thought of the old temptation
to believe in his second chance.

A Veteran of the Great War

It all seems like today: he returns
in the same uniform, on the same trolley,
to the house where his aunt
stepping out into the hallway, her blouse
open to the navel, is the woman he once
had dreams about. Your father is dead
she tells him. He watches her red lips harden
and drops his bag. He listens to himself
wheezing on the steps, past the figures
his father carved into the banister,
past the old photographs,
and into the bedroom. The green walls
remind him first of his father; then
a green cloud drifts around him,
loosing the insides of his body, the chlorine
and the trenches and the men scrambling for their masks.
He wakes screaming and finds a hand
pressed over his face. It is not the sergeant's hand.

His aunt gives him some water. He wants
to hold her, to hold someone
who feels warm and can make him believe
the six months he has are six months to live.
She kisses him. In the Twenties
and the Thirties, and the Sixties
when he has made his six months
into a lifetime, he remembers
her shade of red. He watches her
move through the green room
and out. A day later her bags are packed.
So this is how it ends, he says.

Later, he confuses his story. Two friends
from the Great War were found in the Fifties,
the two skeletons huddled in the buried trench,
masks in place, their hands over their ears.
One, one of them, he says, is her.
I had an aunt in the Great War, he says.

Each night at dusk if the air is cooler and wet
he comes wheezing dry as a cicada
down the steps and past where she stood
when he dropped his bag: earlier in the day, he thinks,
before his father lighted the porch lamps.
He stares into the warm glow.
His lungs are taking in the wet air.
Yellow drops he coughs into his hand.
He calls together the neighborhood children
and tells them stories in which every day
is today. The portraits on the stairs, the soldiers,
are real people; they are children who believe
like he does, in today, and today, and today.

II

A Child in the Pantry

In the dry smells of dust and flour,
in the tang of apples, he finds
something to care for.
Behind the walls
of glass jars in their calm
worlds of color, the tomatoes
and carrots listen
to his story about the vegetables.
In the garden it was raining.
They came to life and danced.

The big table in the kitchen
is the center of Christmas.
His grandchildren listen
to the story that becomes his way
of finding names for them.
It's raining. They're playing
in the garden. The little cabbage,
the potato, the red-as-a-face
tomato. Some have eyes. Some have ears.
They all touch hands and dance.

His parents are gone, creaking
upstairs into their separate beds.
The pantry is cold, quiet. In the dark
the shelves might go up forever.
Dream after dream
waits to be opened
(a glass jar, a story) in the names
of children. The lopped-off
vegetables dance in their juices.
They touch hands like ice.

Dinner Comes Soon Enough

One grandchild is sick to his stomach.
What's that smell? he whispers.
Someone finds the box of eggs under the sink.

The last time they came I had the chairs
in the basement, for painting, I told them.
Each month they come, they eat, and they go.

I tell them I looked days for a needle
and found those letters I never mailed.
I found the cat, stiff and dried in the closet.

I would never take fever like the cat
and crawl into a corner where the old clothes
soak in my smells.

Lemon peels, freshly ground ginger
in a pile on the table, all the bright faces
washed and ready for eating.

Outside, my bluejay is squawking
at the squirrels in the oak tree.
It's my day I tell them. Dinner comes.

We Like the Leaves

His scraping in our yard wakes us.
Our window is open. The day is cool
and barely light.
The old man from next door
is raking our leaves.

One day he cut down our peach trees.
Disease, he said.
Another day
he was harvesting our caterpillars,
the fat Catalpas
he claimed were good for fishing.
The wonders which pass

in the early light. We would not guess
except he tells us:
a hundred robins
roosted in our mulberry tree.
He catalogs
the days our plants produce.
He weighs each onion he digs.

When the fuss he makes
over a few weeds
gone to seed in our yard
seems the madness of an old man,
his flower beds
accuse us. We learn to be good
at being guilty.

Last summer he went too far.
He said we're damned fools
for not cutting our two shade trees
to open light for his garden.
We said, you're right.
This morning his raking pulls us from our sleep.
Admit now, a voice says, *I was right.*

The Butterfly Net

One grandchild runs with a net
like an awkward wing. Another asks:

What in their wings gives them color?
A powder no one understands.

Why do some fly south?
They gather by the thousands and die.

He remembers his teacher bringing
her collection of delicate, rare butterflies,

shattering just as the glass shattered
when he dropped them. He remembers trying

to pick them up, and how useless it was.
Holding her best catch, one grandchild rubs

the large blue wings with eyes.
What's that in your hands? his mother

had asked. She couldn't believe
the colors of his powdery fingers.

The Survivor

The summer he is six, a plague
of toads: toads found

floating belly up, their vague
eyes still searching;

toads lounging
in drawers, smothered

under odd circumstances;
and toads fallen

from the skies, each of which
when lifted, falls again.

No one answers
his question:

why toads jump into fire.
They don't know

he prods one until it leaps.
The shriveling skin

spills a red froth
and something amazing:

the heart still beating,
the pulse like a code.

With his clenched fist
he pounds it out.

Rejects from the Greenhouse

The boy is bug-eyed: the duck
stands two storys tall.
How many tons of flowers?
He imagines the bodies of workers
covered with petals,
each color of the rainbow.
Who decides? Who puts them on?
A committee, the old hands . . .
Where do they get the flowers?

Heads bruised, lean stalks cut short,
they wait in cartons, lacking fragrance.

Between the beds of flowers, humming
with bees, alive with birds and crickets,
an old man with a cart
walks down the steaming aisle
of chrysanthemums. Water drips
from the top of the greenhouse,
rain from the clouds that form.

The mystery of it. He would find you
hidden in the back corner
where no one is supposed to go.
He would kill you with his spade.

How many children lie
in the long boxes sprouting?

If you are good, if you grow up
a beauty queen or famous at sports

you can join a float, smell like flowers,
wave to millions.
The wind picks up the skirts of the best.
Heroes are being made, proud veterans
are waving, thinking: when I was a kid
it seemed so large. And it is.
It is the parade in which the baton twirler steps off
a white blaze into the Western sky.

And when it is over
the boy riding the duck's back
holds on for life.
The huge carcasses, the frames
of wire and wood, are pulled apart
for charity. All those petals
are picked up and packaged by girls.

This is not the end, the boy says,
patting the duck's wing,
riding the wood frame that shakes
and threatens to fall. He whoops and spurs.
He swings into a wide arc, scattering flowers.

Uncle Robert's Peanut Vending Machines

They don't play good soldiers
unless at attention or lying dead, rusting
behind his grandfather's tool shed. No wonder
everyone gave them up. Behind the glass
the peanuts have turned green.
A few green pennies jam the works.
He thinks of the family joke, his uncle's fortune.

One holds an ant colony. Shined up
it's worth a nickle to see. His family
crowds into the tool shed, amazed
at the thousands of ants moving under the glass.
They wonder how he has done it.
It's a secret, he says. You have to train them.
He bangs on the glass and they all go crazy.

A Role for the Christmas Play

Small and awkward under his robe
he feels the pins dig through

and wonders why Christmas
has to find him out, perched shaking

on a platform. His mother's hands
shift his wings. He wants to give her more

than words. The other children spin
and flutter, more like moths than angels.

Stars on strings dangle in Mary's window.
Sister Justina prods him up the ladder.

His mother is a small, white face
before the blank faces of the audience

and the dark rows of seats.
His message from God

is the birth of Jesus.
Pleased with the lines,

unsure of their force, he repeats them.
Pins and words hold up the house.

The Pet Cat

He spreads its plum-colored lining
and finds the stomach, larger
than expected, laced with blue veins.

His mother never explained:
what did the cat know?

Her new canary trills in the window.
The screen door bangs like a trap.
His knife in the stomach looses dark blood.

He finds the rumor the cat found:
undigested bones and feathers,

what his mother killed for.
Even if he buries them, his shirt, the blood
and feathers, she'll find them.

The bloody stains hide nothing.
Nothing he says can stop her.

The Boy in the Terraced Yard

In the highest yard two expanding fig trees
and the bed of strawberries wilt
in the afternoon heat. He lies along the edge
of the goldfish pond and watches
the sunfish eating the bread he holds out to them.

Down toward the house the beds of iris
mimic the colors of the sunfish, turning
in the slight wind near the tool shed,
which has dropped into shade
under the oak trees.

Now he remembers the danger: his grandfather
warning of poison ivy and yellow jackets
nesting in the rocks.
But the memory of the newly caught fish
gliding across the pond, like birds

to peck at the bread he feeds them,
is more dangerous: the face
of his grandfather is straining,
his blue eyes are clouded,
and his hands struggle in the water.

Are they alive? he asks.
On the rock wall above,
the wasps gather. The sprigs
of ivy wilt in the heat.
The boy refuses to answer.

St. Margaret's School

Sister Ann and the new priest
who run and wave their arms toward him
are like the boy's nightmare of his parents
screaming and turning to black cloth.

The bees! They shout: Get away
from the bees in the tree!

The small bodies swirl
as hundreds swarm out:
a depth which seems to the boy
beautiful and frightening.

He hates the nun and the priest.
They think it is a sin

to disobey them, to risk
getting wrapped-up in the bees.
Inside the swarm how do they breathe?
In detention, he prays that God forgives.

Sister Ann has carried a basket and a broom
to the priest. They circle the tree;
their sleeves are flapping in the wind.
Hail Mary Full of Grace, the boy says,

and the bees respond.

The Planetarium

The stars light in the dome
closer than the boy wants.
We will find where we are,
his teacher says.

Who cares, he thinks. The others
pretend they are spacemen on a star
where the jukebox plays for nothing.
The girls all want to dance.

Orion, his teacher says;
his arms and legs are chance;
going to a distant star
we'd see him pulled apart.

The hunter spins against the bear.
A voice says: Follow me . . . .
From their seats the others rise
and whisper they are bats:

disembodied hands
fluttering in the stars.
Children, he thinks.
Not like me.

The Woman Nine Feet Tall

I can feel in the night
how my children are scared
and why they love the day.

I leave their beds
and they dream of death.
I return

taller than their dreams,
and I wake them up.
Ignore the stories, I say,

forget *their* dreams,
their gossip.
Make your own.

My nine feet of bone towers,
my dancing gaits,
are play for them.

Even my husband has a need:
to cure the harms
I shrink from.

Dressing out my bones
on our bed,
he hugs me out of joint.

Go on, I tell him.
Protect me
under the sheets.

I am carried out
into the house. My body
gates and towers
like nothing they have seen.

The Children's Committee

In the shadows of the full moon
mother's foolish dance

the one she calls her dance
of bones. The doctor signs her mad.
He proves what we know.
Those nights she put us to bed we grew
from fear of the dark into her new fear.
Our voices come and go.

We tell her how to live, to know
the taste of a thing is right.
She drives, hearing the dead
and we say don't listen. The lights
turn red or green on impulse. The dead
have nothing to say to this.

This is how we died. We sleep with our faces
under blankets in the back of her car,
not wanting to let her go.
The wheel gives way. And all the fear.
And we give way too.
We lock her where she breathes.

We come and go as we please.

To My Wife

Your mother bumps into everything
and forgets where she is.
She hears your father's voice telling her
trust is for children. I can't trust
my children, she says. Always packing me off.
She sits under a tree and chains dandelions.

The window of her south pantry
lets in a dirty light.
The potatoes have gone bad.
The white, almost clear sprouts
finger the glass. Do you think
you will age like your mother: that image
of her at the wood stove,
a brush of flour on her chin?

Your children have wandered
into the yard with their hands tight
over their eyes. Her bags are packed
and your mother is gone from under the tree.
Finding her has become the game.

In the back seat of the car
she is a small knot of muscle, bent, waiting.
Waiting out her children and her grandchildren.
She is chewing on grass, on something
hidden in her hands.

The Visitors

Under the glaze of the afternoon sun
her room lightens.
The doctor is packing his instruments.

And mother, posing her gown,
is remote; sitting on the windowsill,
she pours water on a flower.

Once, she tells the doctor,
my husband rushed across the room
and pressed a rose in my hand.

In the yard,
our calm, childlike faces look back.
We watch her green gown beating

the window and the white casement.
A spot of paint on a wall of canvas:
the flower is the secret

we have shared for years. We are
like our father's paintings
of acrobats. Deaf and silent,

we throw up our hands.

The Fox

Fox . . . my father said.
Where does it live, how big
is it, what does it eat besides chickens?

Tonight, one crawls
through the crack in my door.
It slides across the pillow.

I repeat God
desperately into the red fur.
Nothing has changed . . .

The fur grows beautiful.
I close my eyes
and the fox leaps inside.

Man in a Triptych Mirror

Touch the glass and feel
on each side

what the girl sees.
Your eyes can find

what she wants
when she wants you.

In the wall
the sound, the dream

of kernels dry as teeth
isn't your only answer.

She never sleeps with you.
She never sleeps without you.

In the morning
the mirror breaks.

The pieces cut
your hands.

The drops gather
into bloody eyes.

A blind man is
crawling the attic.

Hear him bait the walls
with his hands.

The rats have sniffed out
his face.

A tongue goes dry
with a laugh.

The police will ask
was it suicide.

Her only answer was
that he would never sleep with her.

Voyeurs

Again tonight the boy downstairs sings
the song he has written for you. Love,
are you listening? Through our bed
the steady beat comes up.
I imagine his hands
strumming those same two chords.
Like a dancer, you move.
He takes your breath in.

What do you feel in a song this simple?
Tell us. A whisper will do.
Does the music force you
to answer with feeling?
Silence, and a good dancer never talks.
Listen. His song is reaching our climax.
He runs out of breath.
Eyes closed, your lips form each word.

Again, the One-night Stand

Somewhere across the bed
in the dark
she is less and less
beautiful.

He rids her face
of candlelight's
easy romance.
He hardens
her too-soft cheeks,
her bright eyes.
He refuses
to let memories
gutter
like sweet, old wax.

In the hard light
of the searchlights
because he set
fire to their house
he finds her.
Deep in ashes,
in fragments of glass.

Her eyelashes
are painted black.
The scratch of a match
would wake her.

At dawn the woman
he ruins has kept

her familiar face,
those same brown eyes.
Their son waking
in the next room
cries the hard slap
of a dream.

Late Winter Is the Edge

Today I celebrate for Elizabeth,
Elizabeth and her abortionist,
more gentle now, his guarantee preserved
in an olive jar. I celebrate
Saturday. On Canal St. I met a girl
in the parade who looked just like
Elizabeth, her face, the blond hair,
and she moved perfectly. I could smell
her perfume, rich as brandy.
Her hands were old. Her face was made-up.
Together this evening after rain
we played with children on the street.
We pulled down wet branches on each other,
making a game
of staggering the streets home.

The Animals

The pillow under her head
settles his daughter.
The dust falls through the light
and settles
on the book in his lap.

He closes his eyes
and the night changes
to spots,
then leaves,
then leaves waving
in a spring storm with lightning.

The story turns and turns
until the ugly swan is beautiful.

It glides across the pond
under the trees
where shape is neither
a joke nor a cause for pity.
And it happens

in a name.
His daughter's head
sinks further in the pillow.
Each night
he brushes her hair.

If he could change her
she would never change.

Turning beyond her in the dark
and in the face of the window
are the animals of her mobile:
the bear, the swan, the lamb.

When he held her in their dance
his hands were strong.
She touched their bodies
and named them.
If they change, he thinks,
today, tomorrow
they will look and sound the same.

The Night-blooming Cactus

This has little to do with the flower
except for a man on the far side of the room
who has been watching it all night.
To concentrate on it from a distance
helps him understand the dark-haired girl
asleep on the far side of town.

In his meditation he has been
the plant which blooms in the night desert.
He is the survivor in a house
of dead relatives. The victim
of friends and lovers. *They* knew
he would always be there. The flower
is motionless. It will always be

a flower and nothing else, except for the man
who draws it in:
a part of himself which cares
for nothing. The girl might be on the verge
of unfolding a new face
and she would still mean nothing.
He tries to believe what he sees in her.

So the love and the meditation
go on, turning a white sheet and a girl
into a night-blooming cactus.
The cactus unfolds to explain something:
he sees it take on colors,
not of meaning, real colors which mean absolutely
nothing. And that, he understands, is what she feels.